Lullaby and Goodnight

~SONGS AND POEMS FOR BABIES~

Collected and Illustrated by Ilse Plume

HarperCollins*Publishers*

Grateful acknowledgment is made to the following for permission to reprint
the copyrighted materials listed below:
Margaret Hillert for "Lullaby" ("Near and far . . .").
Used by permission of the author, who controls all rights.
Thomas Farber for "Manhattan Lullaby" and "I Swim an Ocean in My Sleep"
by Norma Farber, copyright © by Thomas Farber.
HarperCollins Publishers for "Little Donkey Close Your Eyes," by Margaret Wise Brown, from *Nibble, Nibble*
copyright © 1959 by William R. Scott, Inc., renewed 1987 by Roberta Brown Rauch. Selection
reprinted by permission of HarperCollins Publishers.

LULLABY AND GOODNIGHT
Songs and Poems for Babies
Copyright © 1994 by Ilse Plume
Printed in the U.S.A. All rights reserved.

Library of Congress Cataloging-in-Publication Data
Lullaby and goodnight : songs and poems for babies / collected and illustrated by Ilse Plume.
    p.   cm.
    Summary: An illustrated collection of poems and lullabies by a variety of authors.
    ISBN 0-06-023501-2. — ISBN 0-06-023502-0 (lib. bdg.)
    1. Children's poetry.   2. Lullabies.   [1. Poetry—Collections.   2. Lullabies.]   I. Plume, Ilse, ill.
PN6109.97.L85   1994   93-4425
808.81'0083—dc20   CIP
                                                                                                               AC

1   2   3   4   5   6   7   8   9   10
❖
First Edition

The artwork for each picture is prepared using colored pencil on Strathmore drawing paper.
Book design by Christine Kettner, Elynn Cohen, and Ilse Plume.

Lullaby

Lullaby and good night,
With lilies of white
And roses of red
To pillow your head.
May you wake when the day
Chases darkness away,
May you wake when the day
Chases darkness away.

Lullaby and good night,
Let angels of light
Spread wings round your bed
And guard you from dread.
Slumber gently and deep
In the dreamland of sleep,
Slumber gently and deep
In the dreamland of sleep.

~ *Johannes Brahms*

Golden Slumbers

Golden slumbers kiss your eyes,
Smiles awake you when you rise:
Sleep, pretty baby, do not cry,
And I will sing a lullaby:
Rock them, rock them, lullaby.

~ *Thomas Dekker*

The Star

Twinkle, twinkle, little star,
How I wonder what you are!
Up above the world so high,
Like a diamond in the sky.

When the blazing sun is gone,
When he nothing shines upon,
Then you show your little light,
Twinkle, twinkle, all the night.

In the dark blue sky you keep,
And often through my curtains peep,
For you never shut your eye,
Till the sun is in the sky.

As your bright and tiny spark,
Lights the traveler in the dark —
Though I know not what you are,
Twinkle, twinkle, little star.

~ Jane Taylor

Mockingbird

Hush, little baby, don't say a word,
Papa's going to buy you a mockingbird.
If that mockingbird won't sing,
Papa's going to buy you a diamond ring.
If that diamond ring is brass,
Papa's going to buy you a looking glass.
If that looking glass gets broke,
Papa's going to buy you a billy goat.
If that billy goat runs away,
Papa's going to buy you another today.

~ Traditional

Daisies

At evening when I go to bed,
I see the stars shine over-head;
They are the little daisies white,
That dot the meadow of the night.

And often while I'm dreaming so,
Across the sky the Moon will go.
It is a lady, sweet and fair,
Who comes to gather daisies there.

For when at morning I arise,
There's not a star left in the skies;
She's picked them all and dropped them down,
Into the meadows of the town.

~ *Frank D. Sherman*

Kentucky Babe

Skeeters are a-humming on the honeysuckle vine,
Sleep, Kentucky Babe!
Sandman is a-coming to this little babe of mine,
Sleep, Kentucky Babe!
Silver moon is shining in the heavens up above,
Bobolink is pining for his little lady love,
You are mighty lucky,
Babe of old Kentucky,
Close your eyes in sleep.

Fly away,
Fly away, Kentucky Babe, fly away to rest,
Fly away,
Lay your tiny curly head upon your mommy's breast.
Hmm . . . hmmmm.
Close your eyes in sleep.

~ Traditional

I Swim an Ocean in My Sleep

Night is dark,
night is deep.
I swim an ocean in my sleep.
Night is filmy,
night is far.
I dream upon an ocean star.

Star five fingered,
starry fish
let me dream my favourite wish.

Foam be pillow
for my head.
Ocean billow be my bed.

Dream is dark,
dream is deep,
I swim an ocean in my sleep.
Dreaming deep,
sleeping tight,
I swim my slumber sea of night.

~ *Norma Farber*

Hush 'n' Bye

Hush 'n' bye, don't you cry
Oh, you pretty little baby,
When you wake you'll have some cake
And all the pretty little ponies,
A brown and a gray and a black and a bay,
And all the pretty little ponies.

~ *South Carolinian Folk Song*

Manhattan Lullaby

Lulled by rumble, babble, beep,
let these little children sleep;
let these city girls and boys
dream a music in the noise,
hear a tune their city plucks
up from buses, up from trucks
up from engines wailing fire!
up ten stories high, and higher,
up from hammers, rivers, drills,
up tall buildings, over sills,
up where city children sleep,
lulled by rumble, babble, beep.

~ *Norma Farber*

Baby's Boat

Baby's boat's a silver moon
Sailing in the sky,
Sailing o'er a sea of sleep
While the stars float by.

Sail, baby, sail,
Out upon that sea;
Only don't forget to sail
Back again to me.

Baby's fishing for a dream,
Fishing far and near,
Her line a silver moonbeam is,
Her bait a silver star.

Sail, baby, sail,
Out upon that sea;
Only don't forget to sail
Back again to me.

~ Traditional

Lullaby

Near and far, near and far,
Over the hill there hangs a star.
Over the star is a slice of moon,
And a cloud will cover them very soon.

Far and near, far and near,
My teddy and I are dreaming here
And over us both my mother is bending,
Crooning a tune without any ending.

Near and far, near and far,
Over the hill there hangs a star.

~ Margaret Hillert

Nantucket Lullaby

Hush, the waves are rolling in,
   White with foam, white with foam,
Father toils amid the din,
   While baby sleeps at home.

Hush, the ship rides in the gale,
   Where they roam, where they roam,
Father seeks the roving whale,
   While baby sleeps at home.

Hush, the wind sweeps o'er the deep,
   All alone, all alone,
Mother now the watch will keep,
   Till father's ship comes home.

                              ~ *Traditional*

Seal Lullaby

Oh hush, thee, my baby,
    the night is behind us,
And black are the waters
    that sparkled so green.
The moon, o'er the combers,
    looks downward to find us
At rest in the hollows
    that rustle between.
Where billow meets billow,
    then soft be thy pillow,
Ah, weary wee flipper-ling,
    curl at thy ease!
The storm shall not wake thee,
    nor shark over-take thee,
Asleep in the arms of
    the slow-swinging seas!

~ Rudyard Kipling

Little Donkey Close Your Eyes

Little Donkey on the hill
Standing there so very still
Making faces at the skies
Little Donkey close your eyes.

Wild young birds that sweetly sing
Curve your heads beneath your wing
Dark night covers all the skies
Wild young birds now close your eyes.

Little child all tucked in bed
Looking such a sleepy head
Stars are quiet in the skies
Little child now close your eyes.

~ Margaret Wise Brown